"Brilliantly brings science to life. Anyone who thinks physics is a boring subject needs to get hold of this wonderful book. I guarantee they will quickly change their minds."
Professor Jim Al-Khalili CBE – scientist, author and broadcaster

"Forces of the Day unlocks the magic and glory of physics. Children everywhere will be mesmerised by the storytelling, beautiful illustrations and sense of wonder this magnificent book conveys."
Amol Rajan – journalist, broadcaster, quiz host and father of four

For Mum and Dad, whose love is a constant force. x– S.L.
The World in a Day, for Ample and Zac. – H.H.

First published in Great Britain 2026 by Red Shed, part of Farshore
An imprint of HarperCollins*Publishers*
I London Bridge Street,
London SEI 9GF
www.farshore.co.uk

HarperCollins*Publishers*
Macken House, 39/40 Mayor Street Upper,
Dublin I, DOI C9W8

Red Shed is a registered trademark of HarperCollins*Publishers* Ltd.

Text copyright © Samantha Lewis 2026
Illustrations copyright © Hao Hao 2026
Samantha Lewis and Hao Hao have asserted their moral rights.
Consultancy by Professor Kirsty Duffy and Jacob Breward Butler.
With thanks to Dr Mike Goldsmith.

ISBN 978 0 00 871265 5
Printed in Malaysia.

I

A CIP catalogue record for this title is available from the British Library.

Stay safe online. Any website addresses listed in this book are correct
at the time of going to print. However, Farshore is not responsible for content
hosted by third parties. Please be aware that online content can be subject
to change and websites can contain content that is unsuitable for children.
We advise that all children are supervised when using the internet.

Experiments and activities are performed at your own risk, follow the instructions and
ALWAYS ask an adult for help. HarperCollins is not responsible for the results of your
experiments. Always ask an adult for help with any craft activity or DIY project.
Wear protective clothes and cover surfaces to avoid damage or staining. Adult
supervision is recommended when using any kitchen equipment, including ovens
and other heat sources. Always ask an adult before accessing games or content online.

FORCES of the DAY

Samantha Lewis

Illustrated by Hao Hao

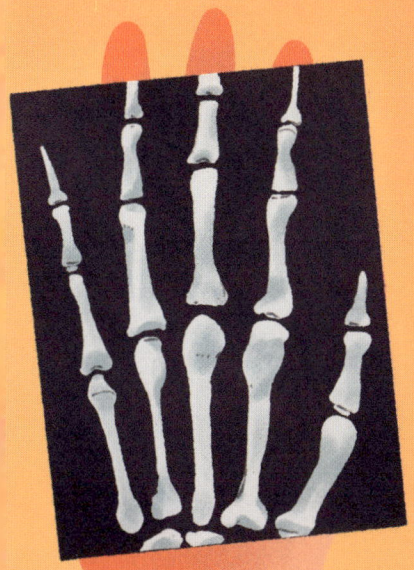

RED
SHED

Introduction

Why are bubbles round? How can you make fresh ice cream in minutes? And what does pigeon poo have to do with the birth of the Universe? To answer these seemingly random and unrelated questions, you need to know about some of the hidden **forces** that control everything around you . . .

Have you ever stopped to think about why things always fall when you drop them (particularly annoying when it's your last bit of chocolate)? Or why a magnet sticks to your fridge? Or why you always see lightning before you hear thunder?

THE FUN OF PHYSICS

Well, there's a whole branch of science (called physics) dedicated to figuring out the rules that explain how everything around you behaves – from physical objects to heat, sound and light.

While rules might not sound that exciting (you may think you have enough of them at school), *these* ones are way more interesting. They've led to amazing inventions and discoveries that make your everyday life more fun – so you can do things like watch TV, make popcorn or listen to music.

FEEL THE FORCE

Although the hidden forces of physics are all around you, shaping your day from morning to night, it's taken centuries of work by scientists to figure out what they are (and they're still working on them now). This book will help you to discover them in every waking moment.

Once you start noticing the effects of these forces, you'll begin to see everything around you in a different way. As you read, you'll also discover clever tricks to help make your day more exciting AND impress everyone you know – like how to spin faster on a roundabout or make a balloon stick to your hair (because why wouldn't you want to do that?).

Ready to start finding these hidden forces and (definitely not boring!) rules everywhere in your daily life? Let's start with a force that makes it tricky to get out of bed . . .

Wakey Wakey

As a new day dawns and you're beginning to wake up, do you know what's keeping you in bed? I don't mean the fact that you don't want to get up for school yet, but what exactly is stopping you from floating up to the ceiling?

GR(APPLE) WITH GRAVITY

According to legend, it was an apple falling from a tree, rather than falling out of bed, that got English physicist **Sir Isaac Newton** thinking about this in the 1660s. He wondered why the apple fell straight down and not sideways – or even upwards.

He realised there must be a force that pulls apples towards the ground – and it's the same force that keeps you on your bed. He called it gravity and recognised it as the force that pulls ALL objects in the Universe towards each other.

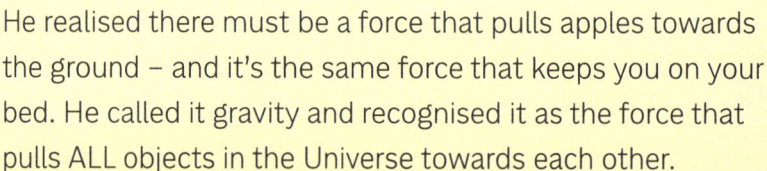

So why doesn't gravity move an apple to your mouth? Well, Newton figured out that the size of the force depends on the **mass** of each object involved. In other words, how much 'stuff' they are made from. However big your apple is, it has a very small mass compared to Earth (and so do you), so the force isn't big enough to pull it towards you.

For the pull of gravity to be strong enough to notice, one of the objects needs to be really massive (like Earth). With our enormous planet involved, the pull of gravity is strong enough to keep you in your bed – or on the floor if you roll off!

COSMIC CAROUSEL

As well as explaining why an apple (and everything else) falls to the ground, Newton discovered something even more astonishing about gravity. Strange as it seems, his work showed that this force is also responsible for why the Moon **orbits** Earth, and why all the planets move around the Sun. But if gravity pulls *us* down to Earth, why doesn't it pull the Moon onto our planet? To answer this, you can do Newton's experiment. It was a 'thought experiment', so all you need is your imagination . . .

Cannon

CLEVER CANNONBALL

Newton envisaged a cannon on top of a giant mountain that reaches beyond Earth's atmosphere, firing balls sideways at different speeds. The speedier the cannonball, the further it can travel before gravity brings it slamming to the ground. With enough speed, the cannonball's path matches the curve of Earth's surface – so it always falls but never lands, just like the Moon!

Without gravity, the Moon would fly away from Earth.

Amazingly, you overcome this marvellous force every time you pull yourself up to get out of bed. What a great way to kick off the day!

While you might still be bleary-eyed, the next thing to notice is what makes it possible for you to see anything at all . . .

Open Your Eyes

When you've managed to prise open your eyes and get out of bed, how do you know what's around you?

THE LIGHT OF DAY

Light (for example, from the Sun or an electric bulb) is needed to form an image of what you see – which is why getting to the loo at night can be tricky without turning on a light! But what *is* light? And how much of it can human eyes detect?

Well, the scientific term for light is 'electromagnetic radiation' and it turns out it goes way beyond the visible light that we see. For centuries, physicists have been trying to understand how electromagnetic radiation behaves. What they've uncovered has completely transformed your day, making everything from the internet and your TV remote control to microwave ovens and X-rays possible.

CHASING RAINBOWS

Sir Isaac Newton made a leap forward in 1672, after experimenting with a glass prism he bought at a fair. When light passes through a prism, all colours of the rainbow spill out on the other side. People believed it was the prism that created these hues – but he proved something more wondrous: white light itself is made from all the rainbow colours.

SEE FOR YOURSELF

Make a coloured disc on card like the one on the left, then ask an adult to put a pencil through its centre. Hold the pencil between your hands and rub together to make the disc spin. Marvel as the colours merge into white!

SEE THE LIGHT

We can see what's around us because objects can absorb (take in) or reflect (bounce back) different colours of light – and our brains create an image from the light that reaches our eyes. A green object absorbs all colours *except* green, which it reflects for our eyes to detect. But there's far more to light than colours . . .

BEYOND THE RAINBOW

In 1800, astronomer **William Herschel** made a dramatic breakthrough. Using a glass prism, he split white light into the rainbow colours and measured their temperatures. He spotted that they got hotter going from violet to red. Next, he did something that would transform our understanding of light. He measured the temperature beyond the red, where there was seemingly no light. Amazingly, this gave the hottest reading of all. He'd revealed infrared (IR) light (see page 42).

This was just the beginning, as we now know there are many other types of invisible light beyond our rainbow – part of what we call the **electromagnetic spectrum** (see pages 42–43).

This incredible array of invisible light crops up in unexpected ways throughout your day – starting with breakfast time . . .

A PIECE OF CAKE

If you imagine all light as a huge, yummy cake, then the light that humans can see is a teeny, tiny sliver. The rest of the cake is there – we just can't detect it with our eyes.

If the electromagnetic spectrum were a cake, it would be infinite (unending) – but we can't fit that on the page. Or the planet!

Breakfast Time

Whether you're a breakfast lover or loather,
get ready to see it in a totally different light . . .

MICROWAVE MAGIC

The speediest way to cook porridge is using microwaves. But what are they and how do they heat food? And what does a peanut caramel bar have to do with it?

Just like the light we see, microwaves are part of the electromagnetic spectrum (see pages 42–43) – so you can think of them as waves (like ripples on a pond when you throw a pebble in) that travel through space and carry **energy**.

Unlike the light we see, microwaves are invisible. But we know they're there, because they can do awesome things . . .

A HAPPY SNACK-CIDENT

In 1945, American engineer **Percy Spencer** was working on a 'magnetron' – a device that produces microwaves to power **radar** systems. When Percy (presumably getting peckish) reached into his pocket for a peanut caramel bar, he made a shocking discovery: his snack had melted into a gooey mess.

Rather than getting upset, he wondered whether microwaves could cook food. To test his idea, he placed corn kernels near the magnetron and . . . POPCORN! A new snack! Before long, the microwave oven was born. If there's one in your kitchen, it's still powered by a magnetron that produces microwaves.

FAST FOOD!

So how do microwaves warm up your porridge? Well, pretty much all food (even if it seems completely dry, like a corn kernel) contains water. Microwaves make the water in food jiggle around faster. As the water particles bump into other food particles, they make them move faster too. This heats up the food and cooks it, so before long – PING! – your porridge is ready.

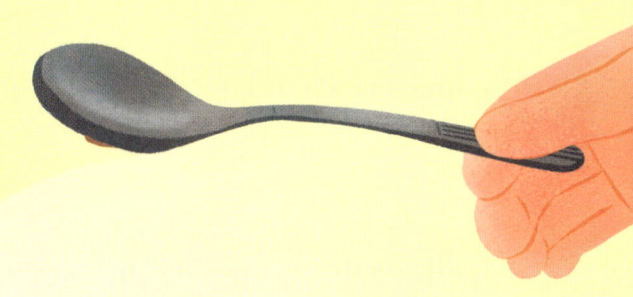

AN EGG-CELLENT TRICK

If porridge isn't your breakfast of choice, then how about an egg? A boiled egg is clearly better than a raw one. But if you had one of each, could you tell which is which without cracking them open? Here's where one of the rules of physics can help you . . .

SEE FOR YOURSELF

Ask an adult for a cooled hard-boiled egg and a raw egg, then spin them. Then gently place a finger on each shell and quickly let go. The cooked egg will stop, while the raw egg will keep spinning. But why?

The answer is because of the conservation of **angular momentum** – which sounds complicated, but it just means that if something is spinning, a force is needed to stop it. When you touch the cooked egg, you are applying a force that opposes the spin – so it stops. But the liquid inside the raw egg keeps spinning, because you only touch the solid shell, not the liquid. So, the raw egg keeps moving.

Once you've had enough breakfast, it's time to get ready to go out. How can physics help?

Get Ready

Whatever the weather, physics can help you decide what to put on . . .

COOL COLOURS

If you have a uniform, you won't get to choose the colours. But when you do get to decide, there's some science to bear in mind.

The Sun gives out all forms of light (see pages 42–43), including invisible infrared (IR) light, which we feel as heat.

White clothes are white because they reflect all the colours of visible light and they also reflect IR. Black fabrics do the opposite; they absorb them. So, wearing white on a warm day and black on a cool day would seem sensible . . .

. . . if only you weren't emitting electromagnetic waves. But you are! Your body generates heat – and all warm things emit IR. White clothes reflect body heat back onto you, so can make you feel hot. Whereas black fabrics absorb heat, so can help to keep you cool.

The fit of clothing (whether it's loose or tight) and the type of fabric also make a difference to how hot you feel . . . so on a scorching day, perhaps just pick what's most stylish – or 'cool'!

FUN IN THE SUN

If it's a sunny day, you probably know that sunscreen is a good idea. But what does it do and how does it work?

Well, the ultraviolet (UV) light that the Sun gives out, which we can't see *or* feel, can cause sunburn.

Sunscreen gives protection because it contains substances that absorb UV light before it reaches your skin. Zinc oxide and titanium dioxide are common ingredients because they are excellent at absorbing UV light.

Some flower petals have UV patterns on them that look great to bees - who can see UV light - but are invisible to humans, who can't!

How bees see this flower

How humans see this flower

Mitten surface area

Glove surface area

KEEPING COSY

On a chilly day, which are best: mittens or gloves? When fingers are tucked up together in mittens, they can share body heat with one another. Mittens also have a smaller 'surface area' in contact with the cold air – so your fingers lose less of their heat. Mittens win! Unless you need to tie your shoelaces, that is.

Before you head off, there are more forces to look out for – especially the ones that can change your appearance . . .

Final Touches

Just a few more things to do before you're ready to set off – and happily, physics can help you to get them right . . .

SHOCKING STYLE

As you're putting on a woolly jumper or brushing your hair, you may encounter a kind of electricity that doesn't involve plugging anything in: static electricity. It won't power any appliances (they rely on dynamic electricity, which need a power source), but it can lead to some shocking effects – and it's caused by electrostatic forces.

Electrostatic forces can either pull things together (attract) or push things apart (repel). But what causes them in the first place?

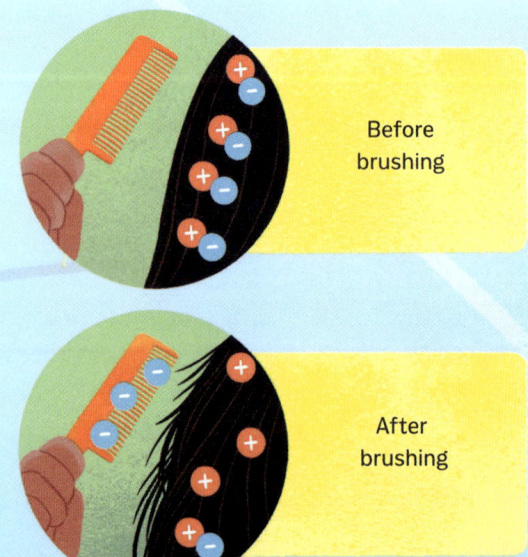

Before brushing

After brushing

CHARGES TAKE CHARGE

Everything, including hair, is made from particles (**atoms**) that have extremely tiny **negative charges** (**electrons**) on the outside. When you pull on a woolly jumper or brush hair quickly, the negative electrons from the hair move onto the jumper or brush. This leaves the hairs with overall **positive charges**.

Charges that are the same repel one another, so the positively charged hair strands push away from each other and spread apart – which can lead to a rather 'interesting' hairstyle. A quick fix is to put some water on the hair, which helps the charges to move around and balance out.

SEE FOR YOURSELF: MAGIC BALLOON

Use electrostatic forces to perform a clever trick. Rub your hair quickly with a balloon to move the tiny negative electrons from your hair onto the balloon. The balloon becomes negatively charged, and your hair is left with a positive charge. Opposite charges (positive and negative) attract one another, so the electrostatic force between your hair and the balloon pulls them together. As if by magic, the balloon should stick to your hair!

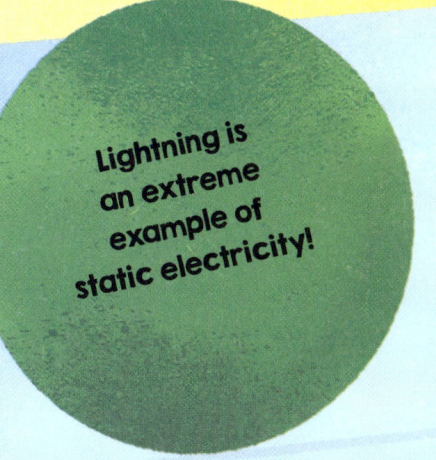

Lightning is an extreme example of static electricity!

TORQUE OF THE TOWN

Before you leave, you'll need to open the door. If you touch a metal door handle after walking on carpet, you might get a little shock. When the build-up of charge on one object becomes too much (in this case, from electrons shifting between you and the carpet), it can cause a spark as it tries to transfer some of that charge to something else (the metal door handle). But whatever it's made of, have you ever thought about why the handle is where it is? It's all to do with another hidden force: torque (or turning force).

When you open a door, you're making it turn around the hinges. How much you can make it move depends on two things – how hard you push or pull the door *and* how far away from the hinges you do that. To get the biggest reward for your effort, you need to strike as far away from the hinges as possible – which is generally where you'll find the handle. If you try pushing the door much nearer to the hinges, you'll see that it's more difficult. But don't waste too much time, or you'll be late for school!

With the door closed behind you, it's time to get moving – and there will certainly be some interesting forces involved . . .

Get Going

Whatever your choice of transport, there are hidden forces that control exactly *how* you move – and every journey can reveal something amazing . . .

BRILLIANT BIKES

Even though bicycles have been around since the 1800s, cycling is still a great way to get around. But how do bikes work?

Over 100 years before the bike was even invented, **Sir Isaac Newton** came up with rules that explain how bicycles (and everything else for that matter) move.

Hop on to discover Newton's laws of motion . . .

NEWTON'S FIRST LAW

Any object will continue to move in the same direction and at the same speed unless a force acts on it.

In other words, everything keeps moving exactly as it is – or remains still – until something is done to change that. So, your bike won't move until you do something to get it going. Enter rule number two . . .

NEWTON'S SECOND LAW

To get an object to speed up (accelerate), you need to apply a force. The heavier the object, the bigger the force needed.

When you push down on the pedals, you're applying a force. The harder you push, the bigger the force and the more you speed up. But as Newton's second law tells us, the heavier the object, the bigger the force required to speed up by the same amount – which is why it's best not to let an elephant hitch a ride on your bike.

Every action has an equal and opposite reaction.

NEWTON'S THIRD LAW

This explains why your bike moves forwards. When the wheels spin, they push back on the ground – so as you pedal, you're actually pushing Earth backwards a teeny bit. Earth hits back with an equal and opposite force on your bike wheels – and that force propels you forwards. Since Earth is *way* bigger than your bike, it barely moves. But you and your two-wheeler go zooming off . . .

Bikes are the most efficient way to travel, even compared to walking! They require the least amount of energy for each kilometre travelled.

If you've got further to go, you may want to switch to four wheels – and you can rely on physics to help you find the quickest route . . .

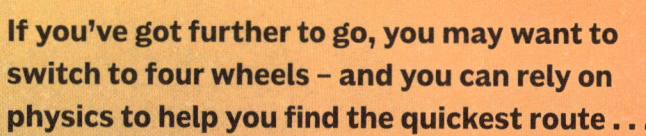

Find Your Way

Plug your destination into a device, and within seconds you can have your path plotted out. But what marvels of physics are key to tracking where you are?

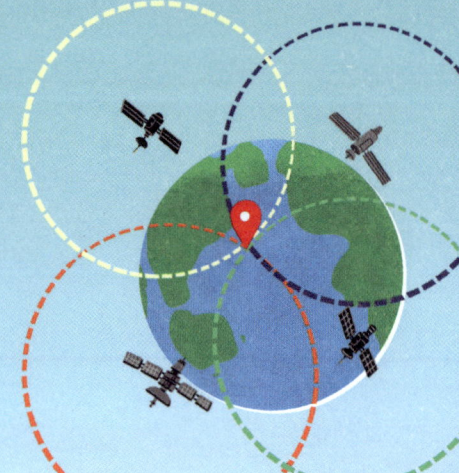

SIGNALS FROM SPACE

Whichever device or app guides you on your journey, it will rely on a setup like the Global Positioning System (GPS) to pinpoint your location. But what exactly is GPS and how does it work?

GPS is a network of over 30 satellites circling Earth from space. These satellites continuously send out signals using microwaves (see page 42), giving information about where they are and what time the signal was sent.

The GPS receiver in a device 'listens' for these signals. When it picks one up, it can work out how long the signal has taken to reach you. Like all electromagnetic waves, microwaves travel at a precise speed (the speed of light), so it can use that information to calculate your distance from the satellite. Using signals from at least four satellites, it can figure out exactly where you are.

PERFECT TIMING

GPS relies on super accurate timing – but physicist **Albert Einstein** realised that some things can make time pass more slowly (and he wasn't talking about very boring lessons). Strangely, when travelling at super high speeds or in places where gravity is stronger, time ticks at a slower pace. This needs to be taken into account with GPS calculations – otherwise you could end up at the wrong school!

Powerful rockets launch GPS satellites into space. They need to generate enough of a forward push force (thrust) to overcome the pull of Earth's gravity and get the satellites into orbit, over 20,000 kilometres above the planet. There, they revolve at over 14,000 kilometres per hour, completing two full circuits of Earth each day.

SHAPING UP

Since Earth is not a perfect sphere, the force of gravity varies across the planet – and this makes GPS calculations even more complicated. Earth's surface is sculpted by mountain ranges and ocean trenches, and its rotation makes it bulge out slightly at the Equator. American mathematician **Gladys West** and her team programmed a computer to make a precise model of the Earth's shape, which is key to figuring out your location correctly – so you can thank them for ensuring you don't get lost!

SCHOOL

Physics should help you get to the right school on time. But what more will you discover in the classroom?

School Time

Science lessons are great for learning more about physics, but you'll be surprised how much you can find out from the other subjects on your timetable – and from one thing teachers ask students to do a lot . . . LISTEN!

BUT HOW DOES LISTENING WORK?

Whether it's a teacher giving instructions or a friend whispering a joke, the key to hearing them is sound waves. These are created when something – anything that makes a noise – moves really fast, or 'vibrates'.

Air is made of tiny particles, so when something vibrates (like your vocal cords when you speak), it causes the nearby particles of air to vibrate too. They then bump into their air particle neighbours and make *them* vibrate, and so on . . .

Air particles pass on vibrations from the source of the sound to the ear.

. . . until the wave of vibrations reaches the ear, where it's turned into signals that the brain can recognise as a sound.

MUSIC MAGIC

Musical instruments make sound waves by vibrating, but how do they make different musical notes?

Well, it depends on how quick the vibrations are. Imagine a race where you and your friends are jumping up and down at different rates, but you all move to the finish line at the same speed and arrive there at the same time. It's not a very exciting race, but sound waves are a bit like that. They all travel along at the same speed – a lively 343 metres per second in air! – but the rate of their vibrations can vary.

Although the speed of sound seems pacey, it's sluggish compared to the speed of light, which is 900,000 times FASTER. This is why you always see lightning (light) before you hear thunder (sound).

High frequency: faster vibrations = higher note.

Low frequency: slower vibrations = lower note.

How many vibrations the sound wave makes every second is called its frequency. Whether it's made on a piano, a flute or a ukulele, a note is a sound wave with a particular frequency. The faster the frequency, the higher the note and vice versa.

On that 'note', it's time for the next lesson, where a legendary experiment awaits . . .

Games Time

When you're out on the pitch, it's important to keep your eye on the ball – and that's exactly where you'll find more forces . . .

PHYS-ICS IN PHYS-ICAL EDUCATION

No matter what game you're playing, it's likely that at some point you'll be required to throw, hit or kick a ball into the air. And I doubt you're surprised that – whenever you do so – the ball comes back down (thanks to gravity).

But have you ever thought about how quickly the ball falls? And does it matter whether it's a tennis ball, a football or a table tennis ball?

THE FUN OF FREEFALL

Someone who *did* think about how quickly things fall was **Galileo Galilei**, an Italian physicist and astronomer, born in 1564.

According to legend, Galileo climbed to the top of the Leaning Tower of Pisa carrying two balls – one much heavier than the other – and dropped them off the side at the same time. Surely the heavier object would reach the ground first? Surprisingly, no! Or at least not without air getting in the way . . .

Galileo realised that – without air – all objects should fall at the same speed when dropped from the same height, however heavy they are – which seems crazy, doesn't it?

On Earth, air *does* get in the way, so a feather falls much more slowly than a hammer because of its shape: on its descent, a feather brushes up against more air particles than a hammer does – so a force called air resistance slows it down.

Long after Galileo's death, astronaut **David Scott** dropped a feather and a hammer at the same time while on the Moon. With barely any air particles in their path, both hit the lunar surface at the exact same time!

Direction of ball movement

Magnus effect force

Air flows faster over the ball on this side

Air flows slower over the ball on this side

CLEVER CURVEBALL

In any ball game, surprising your opponent can give you a great advantage. One way to do that is to make the ball 'bend' away from its straight path, just like the professionals do. The secret lies in something called the Magnus effect. If you're playing football, try to get the ball spinning very fast as you kick it. It takes a lot of practice, but once you've mastered it, you can just relax and watch the magic happen – because the air will do the rest for you . . .

As the ball spins, it makes the air around it move differently on each side – slowing it down on one side and speeding it up on the other. This difference in the air speeds (and resulting **air pressure**) creates a force that pulls the ball sideways as it flies – bending its path and helping you to soar into the lead!

When the school day comes to an end, you may be deciding what to do with your free time. Why not head to the playground and discover some hidden forces that help you have fun?

At the Playground

Whether you're whooshing round the roundabout, soaring on the swings or speeding down the slide, there are plenty of forces at work in the playground.

ALL IN A SPIN

If you don't mind being dizzy, roundabouts are great fun. And if you're a thrill-seeker, physics can help you race round even faster.

After you've got the roundabout spinning, lean in towards the centre and you'll soon be whizzing around at a quicker pace.

But why? When you're rotating, you have something called angular momentum. One rule in physics is that this will stay the same unless another force changes it (see Newton's first law on page 18). Your angular momentum depends on three things: how heavy you are, how far away from the centre you are and the speed you're moving around at.

If you lean towards the middle of the roundabout, your distance from the centre gets smaller. To keep your angular momentum the same, something else has to get bigger. You can't get heavier – so your speed goes up instead! If you prefer to go slower, lean out – but don't fall off!

TIME FOR A (PENDULUM) SWING

As you fly back and forth on a swing, you might be wondering what your superhero name could be. But the same motion, so the story goes, got a young **Galileo Galilei** thinking about . . . physics.

While sitting in a cathedral in Pisa, Italy, he was watching something that behaved just like a swing: a hanging lamp. As it swayed to and fro, Galileo used his heartbeats to time it.

He realised that the time it took to rock from one side to the other didn't seem to depend on how far it swung. Whether it was a gentle sway or a fuller sweep, it still took the same amount of time. He eventually figured out that the only thing to change a lamp's swing time is the length of the wire it hangs from – and that gave him the idea for a **pendulum** clock.

When you're on a swing in the playground, you're like a pendulum – and the main thing to affect your swing rate is the length of the rope. Even the mass of the thing swinging (in this case you) has little effect – which means you could challenge an adult to swing faster than you. So long as the rope is the same length on each swing, you'll both take the same time to swing back and forth!

It wasn't until 1656 (14 years after Galileo's death) that Dutch mathematician and physicist CHRISTIAAN HUYGENS made the world's first working pendulum clock.

What next? How about a trip down the slide?

Down Time

What goes up, must come down – and however you fall, there'll be physics at play.

A BUMPY RIDE OR A SLIPPERY SLIDE?

Gravity does a great job of pulling you down the slide, but there's another force at work that's slowing you down: friction.

Friction is the force that results when things rub against each other – like your clothes and the slide. Too much friction, and your journey down the slide can be pretty underwhelming.

So, how can you make sure that there isn't too much friction getting in the way of your speedy descent? It's largely down to your attire. Synthetic fabrics like nylon or polyester create less friction with the slide than cotton or denim – giving you a speedier ride. But beware! Too little friction and you might go so fast that you land with a bump!

Water slides are so much fun because the water reduces the friction between you and the slide - so you can come zooming down at speed before splashing into the pool!

AN ACCIDENTAL BREAKTHROUGH

Sometimes a playground adventure can end with a nasty fall and – if there's a chance of a broken bone – a trip to the hospital. Thanks to a luckier accident in the 19th century, there's a machine that can check for any damage . . . by making you see-through!

In 1895, German physicist **Wilhelm Röntgen** was experimenting with 'cathode rays' (super-fast streams of tiny particles), when he accidentally discovered invisible light rays that seemed to be able to pass through thick card. He named them X-rays (which sound like something superheroes might use to zap villains, but are actually part of the electromagnetic spectrum – see pages 42–43).

Röntgen soon found these X-rays could go through flesh, but not through bone. He took the world's first X-ray photograph – a ghostly picture of his wife's hand, with her bones clearly visible.

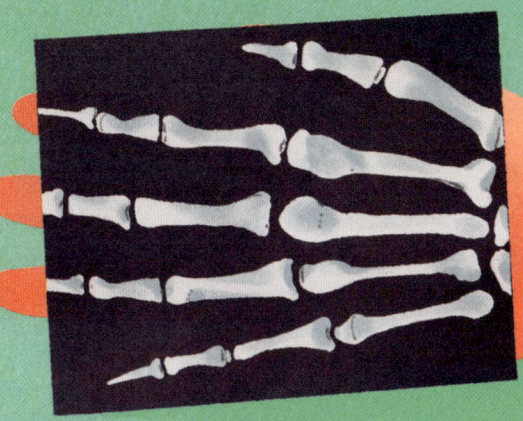

Within a year, X-rays were being used in hospitals to peer inside people's bodies – and they're still being used today to check for broken bones!

Amazingly, X-rays can be used to create images of tiny structures. In 1952, English scientist Rosalind Franklin used them to make 'Photograph 51', which helped to reveal the shape of DNA - the molecule that carries the instructions for how living things grow and function.

When you've finished at the playground, it's time to head home and wind down.

Chill Time

However you choose to relax, there's a fair chance you'll be relying on light beyond the rainbow.

TELLY TREASURE

If you want to kick back and watch TV, then it's good to be in charge of the remote control. With this splendid gadget, you can select what's on – and how loud it is – with the touch of a button. Want to catch up on your favourite series? Your wish is the remote control's command! But how do your instructions reach the TV?

HIDDEN MESSAGES

It's all down to the magic of invisible light. When you press a button on your remote control, it sends pulses of infrared light (see page 42) to your TV. When the TV receives those signals, it can translate them into a command – like 'change channel' or 'volume up' – and respond, while allowing you to remain in the comfort of your sofa.

SEE FOR YOURSELF

Ask an adult if you can borrow a phone. Try pointing the infrared transmitter (at the top of the remote) directly towards the phone camera as you press some of the control buttons. You may be able to see faint pulses on the phone screen, because the camera sensors can detect infrared light.

GAME ON

If you're a gamer, you may like to challenge your friend to an online game (with an adult's permission). Incredibly, it doesn't matter where they are – so long as you can both connect to WiFi. WiFi uses part of the electromagnetic spectrum we came across at breakfast time: microwaves (see pages 13–14 and 42).

When gaming devices are linked up to one another across the WiFi network, the microwaves can transfer lots of information between both devices, coded into a language that computers understand.

As your nail-biting game unfolds, information like player positions and actions is constantly sent back and forth between players. Computers inside the devices translate this information into images that show up on the screen, and sounds that come out of the speakers.

To play a game together in real time, this all has to happen at a super-high speed. And it works because microwaves, like all electromagnetic waves, zip round at the highest speed possible: the speed of light.

If gaming is not for you, there are plenty of other ways you might use WiFi to relax – whether it's downloading music or video-calling a friend or a relative (always ask an adult before borrowing a phone). Next time you do any of these, you can be grateful for the microwaves that are making it possible!

After all that relaxing, it's time for dinner. But what hidden forces are on the menu?

Dinner Time

When you're feeling hungry, food can't come fast enough.
So, how about using some physics to speed things along?

CHOP! CHOP!

Many recipes require ingredients to be cut – and
the chef always needs the right tools (if it's you,
always remember to ask an adult for help).

Think about slicing an onion. A sharp knife is a better
choice than a butter knife – but why? It's all to do with
pressure, which in turn depends on the blade's thickness.
As you push down on a knife, you apply a force. With
a sharp knife, that force is focused onto a very thin area
creating high pressure, which cuts through the onion
with ease. A butter knife has a wider edge, so the same
force is spread over a wider area, creating lower pressure,
which is much less effective (and could delay your dinner).

CATCH-UP KETCHUP

Tomato ketchup is a tasty condiment. But it's a sauce
with a sneaky secret. You probably don't always behave
the same way. I imagine you're *usually* sensible, but
occasionally a little silly. Ketchup is similar. While most
liquids have a thickness that doesn't change, ketchup gets
runnier when it feels a force – and it has a fancy name:
a non-Newtonian liquid, because it doesn't follow
Isaac Newton's rules about runniness.

To get a splodge of ketchup on your plate quicker,
shake the bottle (with the lid on!). The force will make
the ketchup runnier, so it'll flow more easily. Phew!

A SUPERCOOL RECIPE

If you *somehow* have room for dessert, then physics can help you make ice cream in a jiffy! Just check with an adult first and don't touch ice with bare hands.

Pop single cream (120ml), sugar (one tablespoon) and a dash of vanilla extract into a sealable plastic bag. Next, put that bag inside a bigger one containing ice cubes and salt (eight tablespoons). Give it all a good shake for about five minutes, and you'll have ice cream!

One fabulous force in your kitchen is MAGNETIC FORCE, which can either be used to pull things together (attract) or push things apart (repel). Your fridge door closes tightly with the help of a magnet – and you can also use magnets to stick your artwork on it!

How does this work? Well, water freezes at 0°C and becomes ice. But ice isn't cool enough to freeze the ice cream mixture. That's where the magic ingredient comes in – salt. Salt makes water freeze at a cooler temperature. When the ice is mixed with the salt, it needs to be much colder than 0°C to stay as ice . . . so the ice begins to melt.

As the ice melts, it takes heat energy from the things around it – including your ice cream – making them all much chillier. The fancy term for this is 'freezing point depression'. Amazingly, the temperature can drop as low as -21°C, so before you know it, your sweet treat is ready!

Once your dinner's gone down, perhaps you'll fancy a bath – a brilliant place to discover more fascinating facts about the forces around you.

Bathtime

As well as getting you relaxed and ready for bed, a bath provides the perfect opportunity to explore the forces that make it fun.

A ROYAL MISSION

Although it's tempting to fill the bath to the top, you probably know it's not a good idea because the water will spill onto the floor when you get in. But can this everyday fact of physics be useful?

One bathtime (several centuries before you were born) apparently led to a breakthrough that saved a king from being swindled – or so the story goes . . .

In around 250BCE, **Hieron II**, King of Syracuse supposedly asked Greek mathematician **Archimedes** to do some detective work. Hieron had given a goldsmith a certain amount of gold to create a new crown with. When the crown was ready, the king suspected it wasn't pure gold. Had the crafty crown-maker pocketed some of the precious metal for himself and replaced it with a cheaper one – like silver – to make the crown weigh the same?

Luckily, there's a way to find out. Different materials have different densities: even if they weigh the same, they will take up a different amount of space – or 'volume'. A lump of silver with the same **weight** as a lump of gold will be about double the size. So, if the goldsmith had sneakily replaced some of the gold with silver, it would be bigger than expected.

THE NAKED TRUTH

Archimedes could weigh the crown, but working out its precise volume was tricky because of its unusual shape. This is where the legendary bathtime comes in. As Archimedes slipped in to have a soak, he noticed water splash over. He leapt out and ran down the road naked screaming 'Eureka!' (Ancient Greek for 'I've found it!'). He realised that the water pushed up from the bath was exactly the same volume as his submerged body. So, if he placed the crown in water, he could measure how much the water level rises to figure out *its* exact volume too.

When he did, he found that the crown made the water level rise by more than pure gold of the same weight. It took up more space than pure gold – so it definitely wasn't pure gold! The goldsmith had tried to dupe the king – but using physics, Archimedes saved the day!

If you could find a bathtub big enough to fit it in, Saturn would float; it's the only planet in our Solar System that has a lower density than water!

SEE FOR YOURSELF

Does your bath toy float? If it does, it has a lower **density** than water – but if it sinks, it's denser than water. Whilst it's just a bit of bathtime fun for you, some fish depend on the same rule of physics for their survival in winter. Since ice is less dense than water, it floats – so when a lake freezes over, the ice forms in a layer on the top, allowing fish to keep swimming in the (very cold!) water below.

Now that the bath is filled with water, it's time to add soap into the mix . . .

Sparkle and Spin

I don't know about you, but I love a bath
that's brimming with . . .

. . . BLISSFUL BUBBLES

But what exactly *are* bubbles? And why are they round?

Put simply, a bubble is air wrapped up in a thin film of soapy
water. The particles of the soapy water are attracted to each
other, and this creates a hidden force called **surface tension**.
It's this force that controls the bubble's shape.

The surface tension pulls on the bubble's
skin, making it shrink to the smallest possible
size it can be while still holding the air inside
it. The shape that has the smallest amount
of surface (called 'surface area') for any given
amount of stuff just so happens to be . . .
a perfect sphere, and that's why bubbles
are ball shaped!

In your bath, you probably see lots of bubbles
stuck together – and it's the same force at
work. Once again, the surface tension drives
the soapy film to be as small as possible.
When there's more than one bubble, they
can huddle together and share a wall – which
makes their surface even smaller. Clever, eh?

WHIRLING WATER

It's sad when bathtime ends, but there's a fun consolation: watching the water swirl down the drain. Now, you may have heard that the direction the water spins down the plughole depends on which hemisphere you're in (so in the UK it spirals one way, while in Australia it goes the opposite way). But is this true?

Well, things that travel large distances around Earth – like winds and ocean currents – are indeed knocked off course because of the planet's rotation.

An ocean current taking warm water from the Equator to the poles gets deflected to the right in the Northern Hemisphere and to the left in the Southern Hemisphere. This is called the Coriolis effect. It also impacts the weather (cyclones spin in opposite directions in the Northern and Southern Hemispheres).

However, this effect is much too small to control which way bath water twirls – so you can't use it to work out where on Earth you are! But you *can* make sure others aren't fooled by this common myth!

Some physicists have studied draining bathtubs to help them understand more about black holes - strange places in space where the pull of gravity is so strong that even light can't escape!

Once you're clean and dry, it's time to get ready for bed – but there are more forces to discover before you go to sleep . . .

Bedtime

As day turns (quite literally) into night, there are still some big ideas to explore.

LET'S CALL IT A DAY

After a long day, it's always nice to snuggle up in bed. But even as you lie there doing nothing, you're actually doing something amazing . . .

Since (I think I can safely assume) you're on planet Earth, you're racing around along with the planet as it spins on itself. A full twirl takes 24 hours, so as long as you're not at the North or South Pole, you're covering some distance – and the further from the poles you are, the bigger that distance. If you're near the Equator, you'll be travelling at a colossal 1,600 kilometres per hour!

ROUND WE GO

As your exact spot on Earth turns to face away from the Sun, the light fades, eventually leaving you in darkness. Our planet's constant rotation is the reason that every day turns to night. But why is Earth spinning at all?

We can thank the force of gravity that forged our Solar System almost five billion years ago and set Earth in a spin. The motion continues to this day because there's nothing to stop it (see conservation of angular momentum on page 13).

INVISIBLE SECRETS

Even as night falls, it's not really dark at all, because as you now know, most light is invisible to the human eye. Though you can't see it, there's still loads of light out there – and it can reveal extraordinary things about our Universe.

Over the last century or so, scientists have discovered more ways to detect invisible light with special instruments. By looking beyond the rainbow, we've been able to peer deeper and deeper into the Universe and discover more of its mysterious secrets – like the infrared glow of regions where stars are born, the radio wave whispers of distant galaxies, and the X-ray streams of strange black holes.

The Hubble Space Telescope orbits Earth and observes the Universe by detecting light from different parts of the electromagnetic spectrum. In 2016, it spotted Icarus - a blue supergiant star so distant that its light has taken around 9 billion years to reach Earth. And you thought that car journey to your relatives was long!

Now, how about a bedtime story? There's still an opportunity for some time-travelling adventures . . .

Story Time

Before you turn out *your* lights, read the tale of the *first ever* light . . . which involves – of all things – pigeon poo!

HUMBLE BEGINNINGS

In 1964, two American researchers – **Arno Penzias** and **Robert Wilson** – were doing experiments with a giant radio receiver (an instrument that could detect even very faint radio wave signals), when they heard a strange and persistent background noise.

Day or night, no matter where they pointed the receiver, they couldn't get rid of it. But what was causing it? Some pigeons who were nesting nearby had done their business in the receiver, so they assumed that the pigeon poo was to blame.

After a thorough clean, it became clear that the pigeons were innocent: what they were in fact picking up was the faint remnants of the very first light that filled our Universe 14 billion years ago, after the **Big Bang**. Amazing, eh?

TIME TRAVELLING SUPER STARS

If you're not ready to sleep, then how about a bit of time travelling before you drift off? If you can spot a star twinkling in the sky, then you have almost everything you need to set off on your adventure. The only other thing required is your imagination . . . because you're actually seeing that star as it was in the past.

Even though light is the fastest thing in the Universe, the starlight hitting your eyes has hurtled through vast distances of space to reach you.

And that's taken lots of time . . .

The light from Sirius (the brightest star in the night sky) has taken just over eight and a half years to get to us. How old were you when it set off? Were you born yet?

Mirzam (in the same **constellation** as Sirius: Canis Major) is 500 **light-years** away – so the light we can see from it now was emitted when King Henry VIII of England was on the throne in the 1500s.

Eta Carinae is around five million times brighter than our Sun, but is so far away (7,500 light-years) that woolly mammoths were still roaming about when the light we can see now began its journey.

Before you close your eyes and drift off, see if you can spot the Moon. It may look motionless, but it's spinning around us here on Earth, held by gravity – the very force that you now know will keep you tucked up in bed until it's time for a new day to begin . . .

Electromagnetic Spectrum

Light we can see – in every colour of the rainbow – is a type of energy that travels in waves called 'electromagnetic waves'. But most electromagnetic waves are invisible to us humans. There are different forms of light all around us – and together they make up the 'electromagnetic spectrum'.

THE LONG AND SHORT OF IT

Electromagnetic waves travel at the same speed, but they behave in different ways – like you and your classmates. How they behave depends on their wavelength. This can be as big as a building or as small as an atom – and the shorter the wavelength, the higher the energy of the waves. Their different qualities make them useful for a huge variety of things . . .

Longer wavelength

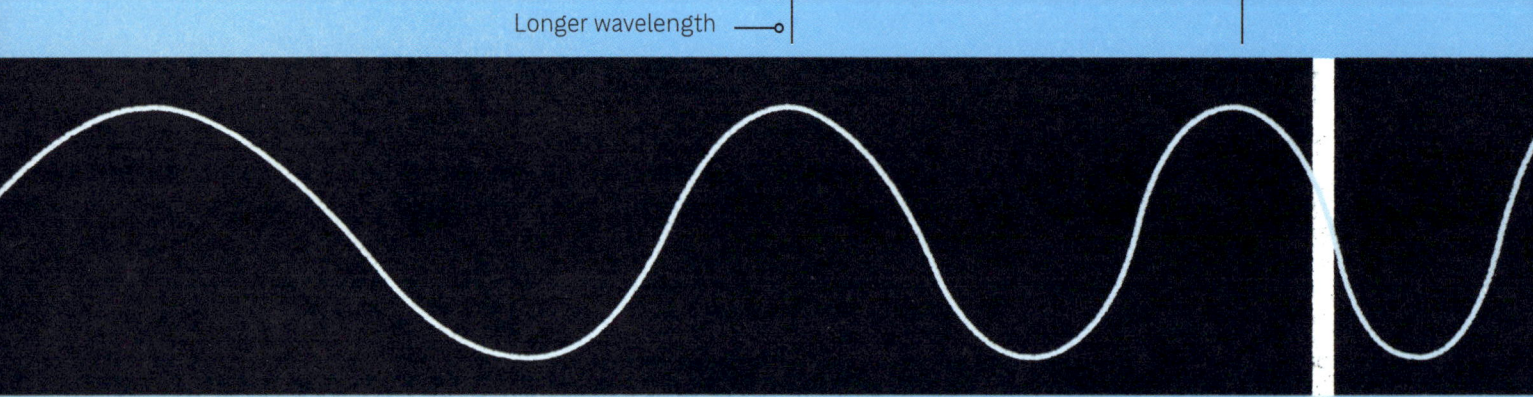

RADIO WAVES

Radio waves can carry information over long distances – so they're used to send radio and TV signals. They're also used to guide radio-controlled toy vehicles.

MICROWAVES

Microwaves can make water in food jiggle around, which heats and cooks it. And they make corn kernels pop (see page 12). They're also used for satellite TV, mobile phone signals, WiFi (see page 31) and GPS (see pages 20–21).

INFRARED (IR)

Infrared waves are released by all warm objects – even you! We feel them as heat and they're used for cooking food in ovens, grills and toasters. They can also send signals to a TV from a remote control (see page 30).

VISIBLE LIGHT

The only electromagnetic waves that are visible to the human eye. We see the various wavelengths as different rainbow colours. Red has the longest wavelength and violet has the shortest.

Unlike sound waves, all electromagnetic waves can travel through empty space – which is why light from the Sun can reach us on Earth. If the sound could get here too, it would be deafeningly loud!

All electromagnetic waves travel at the same breakneck speed of 300,000,000 metres per second – the fastest pace of anything in the known Universe. At that speed, they can zip around Earth 7.5 times in one second.

Shorter wavelength

ULTRAVIOLET (UV)

Ultraviolet waves are emitted by the Sun. They help our bodies make vitamin D, but too much can cause sunburn. They can be absorbed by fluorescent inks in highlighter pens, which then re-emit them as visible light, making them glow. They can also be used as a medical disinfectant.

X-RAYS

X-rays can pass through flesh, but are blocked by bones – so can be used to spot broken bones (see page 29). They can also peer into luggage in airport security scanners and kill bacteria on medical equipment before it's used in an operation.

GAMMA RAYS

In science fiction, they give characters superpowers, but in the real world, gamma rays have superpowers of their own: they can help detect and treat cancer, kill bacteria in fresh fruit and vegetables to make them last longer, and also disinfect medical equipment.

Glossary

Air particles
Air is a mixture of different gases – such as oxygen and carbon dioxide – which are made from particles that are so small you can't see them.

Air pressure
Air particles move at super-high speeds and are constantly crashing into one another and anything they come into contact with. More or faster collisions = higher air pressure.

Angular momentum
Describes how an object is spinning, which depends on its mass, distance from the thing it is moving round, and its speed.

Atoms
Basic particles that make you and everything around you.

Big Bang
Most scientists think that the Universe began as a single point, which began to expand and grow in an event known as the Big Bang about 14 billion years ago.

Constellation
A group of stars visible in the night sky that seem to form a pattern.

Density
How much mass an object has compared to the amount of space it takes up (its volume).

Electromagnetic spectrum
The range of all possible electromagnetic radiation – including visible light – which travels in waves and carries energy.

Electrons
One of the three types of building blocks that make atoms. The other two are protons and neutrons. Electrons have a negative electric charge and whizz around the centre of atoms at super-high speeds.

Energy
Energy makes things happen. It comes in many forms, such as light, heat and electrical energy. Energy can't be created or destroyed but can be converted between the different forms.

Forces
Pushes or pulls that can cause objects to start moving, speed up, slow down, stop, change direction or shape.

Light
When scientists say 'light', they mean all parts of the electromagnetic spectrum. When we say 'light', we often mean visible light, which is the portion of the electromagnetic spectrum that humans can detect with their eyes.

Light-year
The distance that light can travel in a year (around 9 trillion kilometres).

Mass
The amount of 'stuff' an object is made of, measured in kilograms. An object's mass depends on the number and types of atoms it's made from.

Negative charges
One of two types of electric charge. Electrons (part of atoms) have a negative charge.

Orbits
When an object in space moves around another, much larger object in a continuous, curving path.

Pendulum
A heavy object (or 'bob') attached to a rod or string, which hangs from a fixed point and swings back and forth.

Positive charges
One of two types of electric charge. Protons (part of atoms) have a positive charge.

Radar
Radar sends out invisible radio waves, which bounce back when they hit something. The location of the object can be calculated by timing how long it takes for the waves to return. Radar stands for '**RA**dio **D**etection **A**nd **R**anging'.

Surface tension
The pull on liquid particles at the surface.

Weight
The force that pulls an object down because of gravity, measured in Newtons. The mass of an object stays the same, but its weight depends on where it is. An object will have a bigger weight on Earth than it does on the Moon – but its mass will remain the same.

Index